Understanding short narratives from modern fiction

VERLAG LAMBERT LENSING · DORTMUND

Kursmaterialien Englisch · Serie B

Herausgeber: Werner Kracht

Understanding short narratives from modern fiction

Bearbeiter: Egon Werlich

Die im Inhaltsverzeichnis mit ★ gekennzeichneten Texte sind in dieser Sammlung neu. Die nicht gekennzeichneten Texte und Auswertungen sind Nachdrucke aus der *SAMMLUNG LENSING 2 – Text Analysis and Writing Practice.*

ISBN 3–559–**23248**–1

Alle Rechte vorbehalten

© 1979 Verlag Lambert Lensing GmbH, Dortmund

Herstellung: Ernst Knoth GmbH, Melle
Printed in Germany

Die Vervielfältigung und Übertragung auch einzelner Textabschnitte, Bilder oder Zeichnungen ist – mit Ausnahme der Vervielfältigung zum persönlichen und eigenen Gebrauch gemäß §§ 53, 54 URG – ohne schriftliche Zustimmung des Verlages nicht zulässig. Das gilt sowohl für die Vervielfältigung durch Fotokopie oder irgendein anderes Verfahren als auch für die Übertragung auf Filme, Bänder, Platten, Arbeitstransparente oder andere Medien.

Druck A [7 6 5 4] / Jahr 1990 89 88 87

Die letzte Zahl bezeichnet das Jahr des Druckes. Alle Drucke der Serie A sind gegenüber der Auflage 1/79 unverändert und daher im Unterricht parallel verwendbar.

Contents

    1. Barry Hines, "You cheeky young bugger" 5
    2. Alan Sillitoe, "Long-distance running in a Borstal" 10
★ 3. The *theme* of a story (Robert Stanton) 14
★ 4. The chief use of a *plot* (W. Somerset Maugham) 15
    5. Sinclair Lewis, "What's your Ideal, anyway?" 17
★ 6. The *character's* speeches and actions as evidence (Robert Stanton) 23
    7. John Wain, "Got a light, mate?" 24
★ 8. The treatment of *point of view* in a story (Robert Stanton) 29
★ 9. The first-person singular *point of view* in fictional texts (Egon Werlich) 30
  10. Lawrence Durrell, "The change a uniform makes" 31
★11. Aspects of the *setting* of a story (H. Fenson/H. Kritzer) 36
★12. Clues to *symbolism* in a story (M. H. Abrams) 37
★13. Kinds of *symbols* (H. Fenson/H. Kritzer) 38
  14. "Plot, the backbone of the story" (Robert Stanton) 40
★15. Jerzy Kosinski, "Documentary photographs" 45

1. Barry Hines, "You cheeky young bugger"

From: Barry Hines, *A Kestrel for a Knave*. Harmondsworth, 1969, pp. 18–20.

When Billy arrived home, the curtains were still drawn in all the front windows, but the light was on in the living-room. As he crossed the front garden, a man appeared from round the side of the house and walked up the path to the gate. Billy watched him walk away down the avenue, then ran round to the back door and into the kitchen.

'Is that you, Reg?'

Billy banged the door and walked through into the living-room. His mother was standing in her underslip, a lipstick poised at her mouth, watching the doorway through the mirror. When she saw Billy, she started to apply the lipstick.

'O, it's you, Billy. Haven't you gone to school yet?'

'Who's that bloke?'

His mother pressed her lips together and stood the capsule, like a bullet, on the mantelpiece.

'That's Reg. You know Reg, don't you?'

She took a cigarette packet from the mantelpiece and shook it.

'Hell! I forgot to ask him for one.'

She dropped the packet into the hearth and turned to Billy.

'You haven't got a fag on you, have you, love?'

Billy moved across to the table and placed both hands round the teapot. His mother pulled her skirt on and tried to zip it on the hip. The zip would only close half-way, so she secured the waistband with a safety pin. The zip slipped as soon as she moved, and the slit expanded to the shape of a rugby ball. Billy shoved a finger down the spout of the teapot.

'Is that him you come home wi' last night?'

'There's some tea mashed if you want a cup, but I don't know if t'milk's come or not.'

'Was it?'

'Oh, stop pestering me! I'm late enough as it is.'

She crumpled her sweater into a tyre and eased her head through the hole, trying to prevent her hair from touching the sides.

'Do me a favour, love, and run up to t'shop for some fags.'

'They'll not be open yet.'

'You can go to t'back door. Mr Hardy'll not mind.'

'I can't, I'll be late.'

'Go on, love, and bring a few things back wi'you; a loaf and some butter, and a few eggs, summat like that.'

'Go your sen.'

'I've not time. Just tell him to put it in t'book and I'll pay him at t'week-end.'
'He says you can't have owt else 'til you've paid up.'
40 'He always says that. I'll give you a tanner if you go.'
'I don't want a tanner. I'm off now.'
He moved towards the door, but his mother stepped across and blocked his way.
'Billy, get up to that shop and do as you're telled.'
He shook his head. His mother stepped forward, but he backed off, keeping the
45 same distance between them. Although she was too far away, she still swiped at him, and although he saw her hand coming, and going, well clear of his face, he still flicked his head back instinctively.
'I'm not going.'
He moved behind the table.
50 'Aren't you? We'll see about that.'
They faced each other across the table, their fingers spread on the cloth, like two pianists ready to begin.
'We'll see whether you're going or not, you cheeky young bugger.'
Billy moved to his right. His mother to her left. He stood out from the corner, so
55 that only the length of one side separated them. His mother grabbed for him. Billy shot across the back of the table and round the other corner, but his mother was back in position, waiting. She lunged forward, Billy skipped back and they faced up again from their original positions.
'I'll bloody murder you when I get hold of you.'
60 'Gi'o'er now, mam, I'll be late for school.'
'You'll be more than late, unless you do as you're telled.'
'He said I'd get t'stick next time.'
'That's nowt to what you'll get if I catch you.'
Billy ducked down. His mother followed, holding on to the table top to retain
65 balance. They faced each other under the table, then Billy feinted a move forward. His mother dived, at nothing. Billy jumped up and ran round the table while his mother was still full stretch on the floor.
'Billy come back! Do you hear? I said come back!'
He whipped the kitchen door open and ran out into the garden. He was half-way
70 down the path when his mother appeared, panting and jabbing her finger at him.
'Just you wait lad! Just you wait 'til tonight!'

I. Notes on the text

The text from Barry Hines' novel constitutes a division which is almost complete in itself. What the reader should know, however, to understand the narrated incident more thoroughly is that Billy returns home (see. ll. 1ff.) after his early-morning paper round, long before he leaves for school. The money he earns by taking newspapers around goes into food for his pet, a kestrel (Turmfalke) which he is training. As to the family, it may be noted that Billy's father left his mother when Billy was a small boy because she had been unfaithful to her husband.

The author was born in 1939 in the mining village of Hyland Common, near Barnsley. After grammar school, he took up various practical jobs before entering Loughborough Training College where he studied Physical Education for three years. After completing this course, he taught physical education for two years in a comprehensive school, south of London. He then returned to the North. His first novel, *The Blinder,* was published in 1966.

II. Words

avenue ['ævinjuː] n.: (here:) wide street with buildings on one or both sides – *Reg* [redʒ]: Christian name, short for *Reginald* – *bang* v.: shut noisily – *underslip* n.: skirt worn under a woman's dress (Unterrock) – *poise* v.: hold in balance – *apply* v.: (of lipstick) put on – *bloke* [bləuk] n.: fellow (Kerl) – *capsule* ['kæpsjuːl] n.: small case – *bullet* ['bulit] n.: small ball such as fired from a pistol – *mantelpiece* ['mæntlpiːs] n.: ornamental structure over and around a fireplace (Kaminsims) – *hearth* [hɑːθ] n.: the floor of a fireplace or the area immediately in front of a fireplace – *fag* n.: (slang) cigarette – *zip* v.: (den Reißverschluß zuziehen) – *waistband* ['weistbænd] n.: (Bund) – *shove* [ʃʌv] v.: push – *spout* [spaut] n.: (here:) narrow tube through which the tea is poured out (Tülle, Schnauze) – *mash tea*: (Northern English) make tea – *pester* v.: make angry with repeated questions, etc. (belästigen) – *crumple* v.: press together into folds (zusammenrollen) – *tyre* ['taiə] n.: (Reifen) – *ease (one's head) through*: put (one's head) through slowly and carefully – *summat* ['sʌmət] indef. pron.: (Northern English) something – *your sen* refl. pron.: (Northern English) yourself – *owt* [ɔːt] *else*: (Northern English) anything else – *tanner* ['tænə] n.: sixpence (before decimalization) – *swipe at* v.: hit at with a swinging blow – *flick (one's head) back* v.: throw (one's head) back with a sudden movement – *cheeky* ['tʃiːki] a.: (frech, unverschämt) – *bugger* ['bʌgə] n.: vulgar term of abuse (etwa: Schuft, Halunke) – *grab for s.o.* v.: try to seize s.o. suddenly – *lunge forward* [lʌndʒ] v.: make a sudden movement forward with the body – *skip back* v.: jump back with a short hop – *face up* v.: confront resolutely – *gi'o'er* v.: (Northern English; informal spoken language) *give over* (slang): stop – *nowt* [nɔːt] indef. pron.: (Northern English) nothing – *duck down* v.: bend down quickly – *retain balance*: (das Gleichgewicht behalten) – *feint* [feint] v.: make a deceptive movement (vortäuschen) – *whip open* v.: push open suddenly or quickly – *pant* [pænt] v.: take short, quick breaths – *jab at* v.: push at with force.

III. Key terms for detailed field study of words (semantic fields, collocations)

The following key terms may be used in order to group systematically the most important word material of the present text for more efficient word learning:

1. *architecture*: the house
2. *man*: movement
3. *man*: clothes

IV. Suggestions for guided analysis and practice

> **Content**   The situation

Analysis

1. What does the opening description of the place that Billy returns to (ll. 1–5) tell you about his social background?
2. Why does his mother mistake Billy for Reg when he enters the house?
3. What does Billy's question about the man (see l. 11: "Who's that bloke?") reveal about the situation?

Practice

4. What does his mother's non-linguistic reaction to Billy's question (see 3) imply (see ll. 12 f.: "His mother pressed her lips together and stood the capsule, like a bullet, on the mantelpiece")? Give a text interpretation.

> **Content**   The mother

Analysis

5. What impression of Billy's mother is created through the way in which the different stages of her getting dressed are presented in the text?
6. What strikes you in the way the mother talks to her son about the cigarettes (see l. 18: "You haven't got a fag on you, have you, love?")?
7. How can the mother's behaviour be interpreted when she tries to make Billy "run up to t'shop for some fags"?
8. How does the mother behave when Billy rejects her efforts with "I don't want a tanner. I'm off now"?

Practice

9. Why, do you think, does the mother not succeed when she orders her son to "get up to that shop"? Write an explanatory comment.
10. What attitude does the mother reveal when calling her son a "cheeky young bugger" (ll. 53 f.) and saying, "I'll bloody murder you when I get hold of you" (l. 59)? Write an explanatory comment.

> **Content**   The son

Analysis

11. Twice in the text "the house" that Billy has returned to is referred to as "home" (see l. 1: "When Billy arrived *home* . . ."; and l. 24: "Is that him you come *home* wi' last night?"). What in Billy's behaviour illustrates his view of "home"?
12. What kind of behaviour does his mother force upon her son?

Practice

13. Against the background of your previous interpretation, how would you characterize Billy's situation at the end of his fight with his mother:
"He whipped the kitchen door open and ran out into the garden. He was halfway down the path when his mother appeared, panting and jabbing her finger at him.
'Just you wait lad! Just you wait 'til tonight!'"?
Write a comment.

| Composition |

Analysis

14. From the *text structural* point of view, how would you characterize the sequence of the stages in which the narrated incident develops?

15. The whole text may be characterized more thoroughly (see also 14) as a "*plotted* narrative" since it ultimately rests on "a sequence of *antithetically* related cause-and-effect relationships among the narrated changes" (cf. E. Werlich, *A Text Grammar of English,* Heidelberg, 1976 (UTB 597), § 82.3). What, would you say, are the antithetically opposed forces in the present narrative which set the sequence of causes and effects going? Fill in the blanks of the diagram of a *chain of causes and effects* below to illustrate your answer with examples from the beginning of the story.

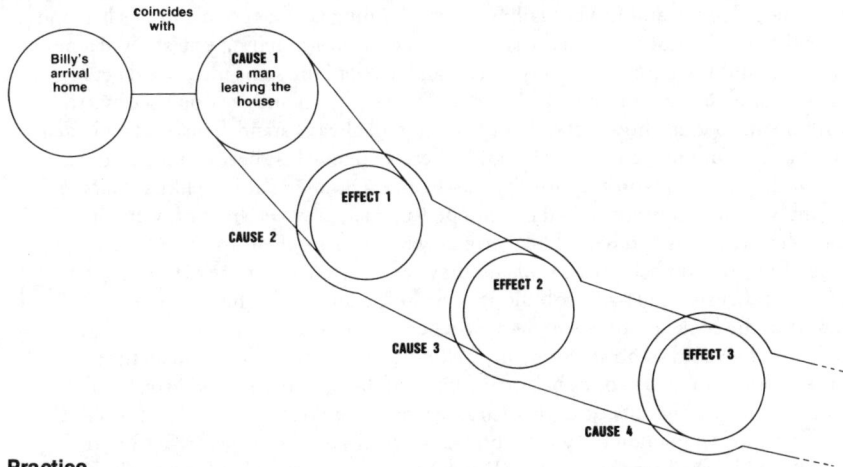

Practice

16. Which direct-speech sentences from the climactic division of the narrative might one quote to illustrate the irreconcilable opposition of the two sides? Give reasons for your choice.

17. How is the chain of causes and effects terminated in this narrative?

2. Alan Sillitoe, Long-distance running in a Borstal

From: Alan Sillitoe, *The loneliness of the long-distance runner*. New York: Signet, 1959, pp. 7–8.

As soon as I got to Borstal they made me a long-distance cross-country runner. I suppose they thought I was just the build for it because I was long and skinny for my age (and still am) and in any case I didn't mind it much, to tell you the truth, because running had always been made much of in our family, especially running away from the police. I've always been a good runner, quick and with a big stride as well, the only trouble being that no matter how fast I run, and I did a very fair lick even though I do say so myself, it didn't stop me getting caught by the cops after that bakery job.

You might think it a bit rare, having long-distance cross-country runners in Borstal, thinking that the first thing a long-distance runner would do when they set him loose at them fields and woods would be to run as far away from the place as he could get on a bellyful of Borstal slumgullion – but you're wrong, and I'll tell you why. The first thing is that them bastards over us aren't as daft as they most of the time look, and for another thing I am not so daft as I would look if I tried to make a break for it on my long-distance running, because to abscond and then get caught is nothing but a mug's game, and I'm not falling for it. Cunning is what counts in this life, and even that you've got to use in the slyest way you can; I'm telling you straight: they're cunning, and I'm cunning. If only 'them' and 'us' had the same ideas we'd get on like a house on fire, but they don't see eye to eye with us and we don't see eye to eye with them, so that's how it stands and how it will always stand. The one fact is that all of us are cunning, and because of this there's no love lost between us. So the thing is that they know I won't try to get away from them: they sit there like spiders in that crumbly manor house, perched like jumped-up jackdaws on the roof, watching out over the drives and fields like German generals from the tops of tanks. And even when I jog-trot on behind a wood and they can't see me anymore they know my sweeping-brush head will bob along that hedge-top in an hour's time and that I'll report to the bloke on the gate. Because when on a raw and frosty morning I get up at five o'clock and stand shivering my belly off on the stone floor and all the rest still have another hour to snooze before the bells go, I slink downstairs through all the corridors to the big outside door with a permit running-card in my fist, I feel like the first and last man on the world, both at once, if you can believe what I'm trying to say. I feel like the first man because I've hardly got a stitch on and am sent against the frozen fields in a shimmy and shorts – even the first poor bastard dropped on to the earth in midwinter knew how to make a suit of leaves, or how to skin a pterodactyl for a topcoat. But there I am, frozen stiff, with nothing to get me warm except a couple of hours' long-distance running before breakfast, not even a slice of bread-and-sheepdip. They're training me up fine for the big sports day when all the

pig-faced snotty-nosed dukes and ladies – who can't add two and two together and would mess themselves like loonies if they didn't have slavies to beck-and-call – come and make speeches to us about sports being just the thing to get us leading an
40 honest life and keep our itching finger-ends off them shop locks and safe handles and hairgrips to open gas meters. They give us a bit of blue ribbon and a cup for a prize after we've shagged ourselves out running or jumping, like race horses, only we don't get so well looked-after as race horses, that's the only thing.

I. Notes on the text

The text forms the introductory division of Sillitoe's long short story "The loneliness of the long-distance runner". The story gave the title to the writer's first collection of nine short stories (1959).
Sillitoe, the son of a tannery worker (Gerber), was born in Nottingham in 1928, worked in factories from the age of 14 and started to write after the Second World War. He won immediate fame with the publication in 1958 of his first novel, *Saturday Night and Sunday Morning*. The novel tells of a young worker who lives for drink and women on Saturday night to free himself from the disillusioning factory work during the week.

II. Words

Borstal n.: place where young offenders live and receive training which is intended to reform them; named after the first such institution at Borstal in Kent – *build* n.: (Figur, Körperbau) – *skinny* a.: very thin – *stride* n.: long step – *do a fair lick*: (slang) run at a great pace – *cop* n.: (slang) policeman – *a bellyful of*: more than enough of – *slumgullion* n.: (slang) inferior, mass-produced food; rations – *bastard* n.: term of abuse for a man – *daft* [dɑːft] a.: foolish, weak-minded – *make a break for it*: attempt to escape – *abscond* v.: go away secretly – *a mug's game*: s.th. unlikely to bring reward or profit – *fall for s.th.* v.: give in to the attractions of (especially when deceived) – *cunning* n. and a.: (being) clever at deceiving – *sly* a.: deceitful (verschlagen) – *get on like a house on fire*: live very well with – *see eye to eye with*: have identical views – *spider* n.: (Spinne) – *crumbly* a.: easily broken into very small pieces – *manor house* n.: area of land with a principal residence (Landsitz) – *perch* v.: sit down on a high resting-place – *jumped-up* a.: conceited, impudent – *jackdaw* n.: bird of the crow family (Dohle) – *drive* n.: road leading to a house – *jog-trot* v.: run at a slow steady pace – *bob* v.: move up and down – *hedge* n.: row of bushes, forming a boundary for a field, garden, etc. – *bloke* n.: (slang) man – *shiver* v.: shake with cold – *belly* n.: (Bauch) – *snooze* v.: (coll.) take a short sleep – *slink* v.: move away in a sneaking manner – *hardly got a stitch on*: (kaum einen Faden am Leibe tragen) – *shimmy* n.: (slang) undergarment worn on the upper part of the body next to the skin – *pterodactyl* [ˌterəʊˈdæktɪl] n.: extinct order of flying reptiles – *topcoat* n.: overcoat – *sheepdip* n.: a liquid containing disinfectants into which sheep are immersed for a few moments in order to cleanse and disinfect their wool and skin; here used to refer to a kind of fat – *snotty-nosed* a.: (rotznasig) –

mess v.: make dirty – *loony* n.: (slang) madman – *slavey* n.: (coll.) servant-girl – *to beck-and-call*: ready to give instant obedience to – *itch* v.: (jucken) – *lock* n.: device for fastening a door, box, etc. – *handle* n.: part of an object by which it may be held in the hand – *hair-grip* n.: (Haarklemme) – *gas meter* [ˈmiːtə] n.: apparatus which records the amount of gas which passes through it; in rented rooms and flats in England gas is often paid for by inserting a coin in the slot of the gas meter. Since gas meters thus hold a certain amount of money they may be broken open – *ribbon* n.: narrow band of fine cloth (Band) – *shag oneself out* v.: (coll.) tire oneself out.

III. Key terms for detailed field study of words (semantic fields, collocations)

The following terms may be used in order to group systematically the most important word material of the text for more efficient word learning:

1. *sport*: athletics

2. *law*: custody

3. *man*: the mind (intelligence)

IV. Suggestions for guided analysis and practice

| Content | The narrator's situation

Analysis

1. The text gives only a few indirect clues as to the narrator's situation and background. Which references are these and what do they tell the reader?
2. How, according to the youth's story, does the place affect his life?

Practice

3. In the narrator's view, what are the aims of the institution? Quote the relevant passage from the text and explain it.

| Content | The narrator's attitudes

Analysis

4. What conclusions about the reformatory effect of the place on this youth can you draw from sentences such as the following: "They give us a bit of blue ribbon and a cup for a prize after we've shagged ourselves out running or jumping, like race horses, only we don't get so well looked-after as race-horses, that's the only thing" (ll. 41ff.)?
5. Where, in his use of language, does the narrator most clearly reveal his attitude to his custodians?
6. What reasons can you find in the text for the narrator's attitude to the authorities?

12

Practice

7. How does the youth's comment from further on in Sillitoe's story elucidate (erhellen) this view:
 "I think more on the little speech the governor made when I first came. Honesty. Be honest. [...] It's like saying: Be dead, like me, and then you'll have no more pain of leaving your nice slummy house for Borstal or prison. Be honest and settle down in a cosy six pounds a week job. Well, even with all this long-distance running I haven't yet been able to decide what he means by this, although I'm just about beginning to – and I don't like what it means. Because after all my thinking I found that it adds up to something that can't be true about me, being born and brought up as I was" (loc. cit., p. 13)? Write a text interpretation of this passage.
8. What, do you think, may have been Alan Sillitoe's intention in creating this Borstal youth? Write a comment.
9. Do you think that Sillitoe's characterization of the social situation in Britain still applies? Write a comment.

> Style

Analysis

10. Which expressions or grammatical forms in the narrator's use of language are characteristic of his social background? Quote some examples and comment on their effect in communication.
11. In most of his sentences, the narrator either refers to himself in the Subject slot (see "I") or to the Borstal authorities (see "they"). Draw up a list of the basic patterns of sentences with "I" as opposed to sentences with "they" as Subject.
12. What grammatical difference can one recognize in most of these sentences?

Practice

13. In what way, do you think, is the narrator's situation reflected in the listed grammatical patterns (see 11 and 12)? Write an explanatory comment.
14. In what way is this impression of the narrator's situation enhanced by his consistent use of "they" when referring to his custodians?

> Text type

Practice

15. In what way, do you think, does the fact that this text is fictional contribute to its influence on the contemporary reader? Write a comment.

3. The theme of a story

From: Robert Stanton, *An Introduction to Fiction*. New York, 1965; pp. 4f.

1 ... the theme of a story is seldom a moral admonition or a piece of useful advice, like "Honesty is the best policy" or "Work hard and you will succeed." Few serious authors aim at improving their readers' morals, any more than at increasing their vocabularies or raising their social positions. Authors use as themes whatever has given
5 their experience meaning. A theme may take the form of a generalization about life, a generalization that may or may not imply a moral judgment. A theme may be a single fact of human experience that the story describes or explores: courage, disillusion, old age. The theme may even be the personality of one of the characters. About the only safe generalization we can make concerning the theme is that it gives unity to the story
10 and meaning to the events.
What bothers most readers is not the presence of the theme or its particular nature, but the fact that it is implicit. They ask, "Why can't the author *say* what he means? Why isn't the theme obvious? Why is it almost always 'hidden'?" In spite of what we may suspect, the answer to these questions is not that authors are compulsively cryptic.
15 Indeed, their task would be much easier if they could first state the facts and then, in so many words, tell us what they mean. But this would be nothing like human experience. The meaning of an experience is to its facts as the color of an object is to its shape; we perceive them together, simultaneously, not as two separate parts of the event. If you have ever compared your high-school annual with that of another school,
20 you know how different the portraits appear in the two books. In yours, you see photographs of people, with recognizable personalities; in the other, you see blank, meaningless faces. The reason is that only part of what you see in your annual is in the photograph; the rest, the meaning of the photograph, is contributed by your memory. But the experience feels like a single act of sight – not like sight plus memory.
25 Similarly, when you see a good friend, you do not look at him and then think, "I like him." You simply see him as a likeable person. If the writer, therefore, is to create an illusion of life, he cannot state his theme in a separate paragraph; he must fuse fact and theme into a single experience. The theme must appear *within* the facts, and it is our job to find it there.

Annotations

admonition [ˌædməuˈniʃən] n.: (Ermahnung) – *bother* v.: (bekümmern) – *implicit* [imˈplisit] a.: (unausgesprochen) – *compulsively* [kəmˈpʌlsivli] adv.: (zwangsweise) – *cryptic* [ˈkriptik] a.: (rätselhaft, dunkel) – *annual* [ˈænjuəl] n.: (Jahrbuch) – *blank* a.: (leer) – *fuse* v.: (verschmelzen, vereinigen).

Suggestions for discussion

1. What would you consider to be the *theme* of Barry Hines' "'You cheeky young bugger'"?
2. Which of the explanations of what a *theme* "may be" would you choose for Barry Hines' "'You cheeky young bugger'"?
3. What different explanation could you choose for Allan Sillitoe's "Long-distance running in a Borstal"?
4. How could you explain the observation that the writer "must fuse fact and theme into a single experience. The theme must appear *within* the facts" (ll. 27f.)? Take your illustrations from Hine's or Sillitoe's narratives.
5. If you consider the youthful characters in both narratives, what *general theme* do they embody? Consider the age of the main characters.

4. The chief use of a plot

From: W. Somerset Maugham, *The Summing Up*. Harmondsworth, 1963 (1938), pp. 145–147.

As a writer of fiction I go back, through innumerable generations, to the teller of tales round the fire in the cavern that sheltered neolithic men. I have had some sort of story to tell and it has interested me to tell it. To me it has been a sufficient object in itself. It has been my misfortune that for some time now a story has been despised by the sophisticated. I have read a good many books on the art of fiction and all ascribe very small value to the plot. (In passing I should like to say that I cannot understand the sharp distinction some clever theorists make between story and plot. A *plot* is merely the pattern on which the story is arranged.) From these books you would judge that it is only a hindrance to the intelligent author and a concession that he makes to the stupid demands of the public. Indeed, sometimes you might think that the best novelist is the essayist, and that the only perfect short stories have been written by Charles Lamb and Hazlitt.
But the delight in listening to stories is as natural to human nature as the delight in looking at the dancing and miming out of which drama arose. That it exists unimpaired is shown by the vogue of the detective novel. The most intellectual persons read them, with condescension of course, but they read them; and why, if not because the psychological, the pedagogic, the psychoanalytic novels which alone their minds

approve do not give them the satisfaction of this particular need? There are a
number of clever writers who, with all sorts of good things in their heads to say and a
gift for creating living people, do not know what on earth to do with them when they
have created them. They cannot invent a plausible story. Like all writers (and in all
writers there is a certain amount of humbug) they make a merit of their limitations and
either tell the reader that he can imagine for himself what happens or else berate him
for wanting to know. They claim that in life stories are not finished, situations are not
rounded off, and loose ends are left hanging. This is not always true, for at least death
finishes all our stories; but even if it were it would not be a good argument.
For the novelist claims to be an artist and the artist does not copy life, he makes an
arrangement out of it to suit his own purposes. Just as the painter thinks with his brush
and his colours the novelist thinks with his story; his view of life, though he may be
unconscious of it, his personality, exist as a series of human actions. When you look
back on the art of the past you can hardly fail to notice that artists have seldom
attached great value to realism. On the whole they have used nature to make a formal
decoration, and they have only copied it directly from time to time when their
imagination had taken them so far from it that a return was felt necessary. In painting
and sculpture it might even be argued that a very close approximation to reality has
always announced the decadence of a school. In the sculpture of Phidias you see
already the dullness of the Apollo Belvedere and in Raphael's *Miracle at Bolsano* the
vapidity of Bouguereau. Then art can only gain new vigour by forcing on nature a new
convention.
But that is by the way.
It is a natural desire in the reader to want to know what happens to the people in whom
his interest has been aroused, and the plot is the means by which you gratify this
desire. A good story is obviously a difficult thing to invent, but its difficulty is a poor
reason for despising it. It should have coherence and sufficient probability for the
needs of the theme; it should be of a nature to display the development of character,
which is the chief concern of fiction at the present day; and it should have completeness, so that when it is finally unfolded no more questions can be asked about
the persons who took part in it. It should have like Aristotle's tragedy a beginning, a
middle, and an end. The chief use of a plot is one that many people do not seem to have
noticed. It is a line to direct the reader's interest. That is possibly the most important
thing in fiction, for it is by direction of interest that the author carries the reader along
from page to page, and it is by direction of interest that he induces in him the mood he
desires. The author always loads his dice, but he must never let the reader see that he
has done so, and by the manipulation of his plot he can engage the reader's attention so
that he does not perceive what violence has been done him.

Annotations

innumerable a.: (zahllos) – *cavern* n.: (Höhle) – *shelter* v.: (schützen) – *neolithic*
[.niəu·liθik] a.: (jungsteinzeitlich) – *sufficient* [sə·fiʃənt] a.: (hinreichend) –
sophisticated [sə·fistikeitid] a.: (intellektuell hochentwickelt) – *ascribe* v.:
(zuschreiben) – *Charles Lamb*: (1775–1834) essayist and critic, also known as one of

the greatest English letter writers – *Hazlitt, William*: (1778–1830) a writer best known for his essays, written in an 'ordinary' manner – *mime* v.: (nachahmen, mimen) – *unimpaired* a.: (ungeschmälert, unverändert) – *vogue* n.: (herrschende Mode) – *condescension* [ˌkɔndiˈsenʃən] n.: (Herablassung) – *approve* [əˈpruːv] v.: (gutheißen, zustimmen) – *humbug* [ˈhʌmbʌg] n.: (Quatsch, Humbug) – *berate* [biˈreit] v.: (heftig schelten, ausschimpfen) – *brush* n.: (Pinsel) – *approximation* n.: (Annäherung) – *Phidias* [ˈfidiəs]: (c. 490–430 B.C.) one of the most outstanding Greek sculptors. He directed the construction of the marble sculptures of the Parthenon – *Apollo Belvedere*: Roman copy of the original Greek Statue (4th century B.C.) – *Raphael* [ˈræfeiəl]: (1483–1520) Italian painter and architect, a master of the Italian High Renaissance style – *vapidity* [vəˈpiditi] n.: (Fadheit, Geistlosigkeit) – *display* v.: (zur Schau stellen, darstellen) – *chief concern*: (Hauptanliegen) – *induce* v.: (herbeiführen) – *load one's dice*: (mit falschen Würfeln/Karten spielen).

Suggestions for discussion

1. What aspects of *plot* does Maugham emphasize and explain?
2. In terms of your analysis of the plot in Barry Hines' text (see questions 14ff.), what does Maugham mean by "the pattern on which the story is arranged" (l. 8)?
3. In your terms (see 2), what does Maugham mean by "when it is finally unfolded no more questions can be asked about the persons who took part in it" (ll. 47f.)?
4. What view do you take of Maugham explaining the "chief use of a plot" as "a line to direct the reader's interest" (l. 50)?

5. Sinclair Lewis, " What's your Ideal, anyway?"

From: Sinclair Lewis, *Babbitt*. New York: Signet Classic, 1961, pp. 59–61.

1 He answered telephone calls, he read the four o'clock mail, he signed his morning's letters, he talked to a tenant about repairs, he fought with Stanley Graff. Young Graff, the outside salesman, was always hinting that he deserved an increase of commission, and to-day he complained, "I think I ought to get a bonus if I put
5 through the Heiler sale. I'm chasing around and working on it every single evening, almost."
Babbitt frequently remarked to his wife that it was better to "con your office-help along and keep 'em happy 'stead of jumping on 'em and poking 'em up – get more work out of 'em that way," but this unexampled lack of appreciation hurt him, and
10 he turned on Graff:

17

"Look here, Stan; let's get this clear. You've got an idea somehow that it's you that do all the selling. Where d' you get that stuff? Where d' you think you'd be if it wasn't for our capital behind you, and our lists of properties, and all the prospects we find for you? All you got to do is follow up our tips and close the deal. The hall-porter could sell Babbitt-Thompson listings! You say you're engaged to a girl, but have to put in your evenings chasing after buyers. Well, why the devil shouldn't you? What do you want to do? Sit around holding her hand? Let me tell you, Stan, if your girl is worth her salt, she'll be glad to know you're out hustling, making some money to furnish the home-nest, instead of doing the lovey-dovey. The kind of fellow that kicks about working overtime, that wants to spend his evenings reading trashy novels or spooning and exchanging a lot of nonsense and foolishness with some girl, he ain't the kind of upstanding, energetic young man, with a future – and with Vision! – that we want here. How about it? What's your Ideal, anyway? Do you want to make money and be a responsible member of the community, or do you want to be a loafer, with no Inspiration or Pep?"

Graff was not so amenable to Vision and Ideals as usual. "You bet I want to make money! That's why I want that bonus! Honest, Mr. Babbitt, I don't want to get fresh, but this Heiler house is a terror. Nobody'll fall for it. The flooring is rotten and the walls are full of cracks."

"That's exactly what I mean! To a salesman with a love for his profession, it's hard problems like that that inspire him to do his best. Besides, Stan – Matter o' fact, Thompson and I are against bonuses, as a matter of principle. We like you, and we want to help you so you can get married, but we can't be unfair to the others on the staff. If we start giving you bonuses, don't you see we're going to hurt the feeling and be unjust to Penniman and Laylock? Right's right, and discrimination is unfair, and there ain't going to be any of it in this office! Don't get the idea, Stan, that because during the war salesmen were hard to hire, now, when there's a lot of men out of work, there aren't a slew of bright young fellows that would be glad to step in and enjoy your opportunities, and not act as if Thompson and I were his enemies and not do any work except for bonuses. How about it, heh? How about it?"

"Oh – well – gee – of course –" sighed Graff, as he went out, crabwise.

Babbitt did not often squabble with his employees. He liked to like the people about him; he was dismayed when they did not like him. It was only when they attacked the sacred purse that he was frightened into fury, but then, being a man given to oratory and high principles, he enjoyed the sound of his own vocabulary and the warmth of his own virtue. To-day he had so passionately indulged in self-approval that he wondered whether he had been entirely just:

"After all, Stan isn't a boy any more. Oughtn't to call him so hard. But rats, got to haul folks over the coals now and then for their own good. Unpleasant duty, but – I wonder if Stan is sore? What's he saying to McGoun out there?"

So chill a wind of hatred blew from the outer office that the normal comfort of his evening home-going was ruined. He was distressed by losing that approval of his employees to which an executive is always slave. Ordinarily he left the office with a thousand enjoyable fussy directions to the effect that there would undoubtedly be important tasks to-morrow, and Miss McGoun and Miss Bannigan would do well

to be there early, and for heaven's sake remind him to call up Conrad Lyte soon 's he came in. To-night he departed with feigned and apologetic liveliness. He was as afraid of his still-faced clerks – of the eyes focused on him, Miss McGoun staring with head lifted from her typing, Miss Bannigan looking over her ledger, Mat Penniman
60 craning around at his desk in the dark alcove, Stanley Graff sullenly expressionless – as a parvenu before the bleak propriety of his butler. He hated to expose his back to their laughter, and in his effort to be casually merry he stammered and was raucously friendly and oozed wretchedly out of the door.

I. Notes on the text

The text is an unabridged passage from Sinclair Lewis' novel *Babbitt* (first published in 1922). The novel is about a middle-aged American businessman, his conformist outlook, his limited ambitions as a social climber and his private weaknesses. Many critics have considered *Babbitt* as Lewis's best novel. It is ranked as "the major documentation in literature of American business culture in general" (Mark Schorer, who wrote Lewis's biography in 1961).
Sinclair Lewis (1885–1951) made his impact in the 1920s with novels strongly critical of the commercial aspects of American society: *Main Street* (1920), *Arrowsmith* (1925), *Elmer Gantry* (1927), and *Dodsworth* (1929). In 1930, Lewis was awarded the Nobel Prize for literature, the first to be received by an American writer.

II. Words

tenant ['tenənt] n.: person who pays rent for the use of a building, room, land, etc. (Mieter, Pächter) – *commission* n.: payment to s.o. for selling goods, etc. that rises in proportion to the results – *bonus* ['bəunəs] n.: payment in addition to what is usual, necessary or expected – *con s.o. along* v.: (coll.) persuade s.o. to do s.th. not in his best interest after winning his *confidence – jump on s.o.* v.: (coll.) reprove s.o. severely (jdn. streng tadeln) – *poke s.o. up* v.: (coll.) push s.o. to do more work – *appreciation* [ə.priːʃiˈeiʃən] n.: proper understanding and recognition (Anerkennung) – *property* n.: area of land or land and buildings owned (Eigentum, Besitz) – *prospect* ['prɔspekt] n.: possible customer or client – *listing* n.: (here:) item on a list (Katalogisierung) – *hustle* v.: (A. E. coll.) sell s.th. by energetic (especially, deceitful) activity (Kunden fangen) – *lovey-dovey* ['lʌvidʌvi] n.: (etwa: Liebesgeturtele) – *kick about doing s.th.* v.: (coll.) protest, show annoyance about – *trashy* a.: worthless (Schund-) – *spoon* v.: (coll.) behave in a way that shows that one is in love – *upstanding* [-'--] a.: strong and healthy (aufrecht) – *loafer* ['ləufə] n.: person who wastes time – *pep* n.: (slang) vigour, spirit, energy (etwa: Schwung) – *be amenable* [əˈmiːnəbl] *to*: be willing to be guided or controlled – *get fresh* v.: (A.E. coll.) impudent (frech, unverschämt werden) – *fall for s.th.* v.: (coll.) yield to the charms of, especially when deceived – *flooring* ['flɔːriŋ] n.: boards used for making floors (Fußboden) – *crack* n.: (Riß) – *a slew of*: a lot, a whole group of (eine gewaltige Menge) – *crabwise* a.: like a crab, moving sideways – *squabble*

19

['skwɔbl] v.: engage in a petty (kleinlich) or noisy quarrel – *dismay* [dis'mei] v.: fill with feeling of fear and discouragement – *given to s.th.*: having as a habit or inclination – *oratory* ['ɔrətəri] n.: (art of) making speeches – *indulge in* v.: give way to and satisfy (huldigen) – *self-approval* n.: (Selbstbestätigung) – *rats!*: (slang) Nonsense! I don't believe a word of it – *haul* [hɔːl] *s.o. over the coals*: tell s.o. off (jmd. gehörig die Meinung sagen) – *sore* [sɔː] a.: (verärgert, 'sauer') – *chill* n.: s. th. that causes a downhearted feeling (Kühle) – *distress* [dis'tres] v.: cause great pain to – *executive* [ig'zekjutiv] n.: (here:) person in a business who has administrative or managerial powers – *fussy* ['fʌsi] a.: full of nervous excitement (umständlich) – *directions* [di'rekʃənz] n.: information or instructions about what to do, etc. – *feign* v.: pretend (vorgeben, vortäuschen) – *apologetic* [ə.pɔlə'dʒetik] a.: making a statement of regret (for doing wrong, hurting s.o.'s feelings, etc.) – *ledger* n.: book in which a business firm's accounts are kept (Hauptbuch) – *crane around* v.: stretch the neck like a crane (Kranich) – *alcove* ['ælkəuv] n.: partially enclosed extension of a room – *sullen* ['sʌlən] a.: silently bad-tempered – *bleak* a.: cold and cheerless – *propriety* [prə'praiəti] n.: state of being correct in behaviour and morals (Anständigkeit) – *casual* ['kæʒjuəl] a.: (here:) informal – *raucous* ['rɔːkəs] a.: (of sounds) rough, hoarse (rauh, heiser) – *ooze* [uːz] *out of* v.: pass slowly out of, like thick liquids (langsam verschwinden) – *wretched* ['retʃid] a.: miserable.

III. Key terms for detailed field study of words (semantic fields, collocations)

The following terms may be used in order to group systematically the most important word material of the text for more efficient word learning:

1. *industry*: employment

2. *industry*: the employer

IV. Suggestions for guided analysis and practice

| Content | The situation |

Analysis

1. What is the setting of the talk?
2. What is the talk about?

Practice

3. Before presenting Babbitt's reaction to Graff's request, the narrator tells of Babbitt's remark to his wife "that it was better to 'con your office-help along and keep 'em happy 'stead of jumping on 'em and poking 'em up – get more work out of 'em that way'" (ll. 7ff.). What view of Babbitt is thus created initially? Give an explanatory comment.

| Content | Babbitt and Graff

Analysis

4. After the opening paragraph, in what distinct situations does the narrator present the executive's actions and reactions? Find out the major divisions of the text.
5. What basic expectations as to an employee's work does Babbitt reveal in his talk to Stanley Graff?
6. What view of work reveals itself in these expectations?

Practice

7. How does Babbitt justify his position? Consider sentences such as these, "What's your Ideal, anyway? Do you want to make money and be a responsible member of the community, or do you want to be a loafer, with no Inspiration or Pep?" (ll. 23ff.)
8. What view of Babbitt's justification do you take?
9. What in Babbitt's address is powerful enough to make Stanley Graff give up?

| Content | Babbitt

Analysis

10. How does Babbitt's role differ in the second distinct situation presented in the text (see also 4 above)?

Practice

11. What strikes you if you compare Babbitt's long addresses to Graff with this sentence from the second situation:
"He was as afraid of his still-faced clerks – of the eyes focused on him, Miss McGoun staring with head lifted from her typing, Miss Bannigan looking over her ledger, Mat Penniman craning around at his desk in the dark alcove, Stanley Graff sullenly expressionless – as a parvenu before the bleak propriety of his butler" (ll. 57ff.)? Write a text interpretation.
12. What does the compositional parallelism between Stanley Graff's and Babbitt's retreat emphasize:
(1) "'Oh – well – gee – of course –' sighed Graff, as he went out, crabwise" (l. 41);
(2) "... and in his effort to be casually merry he stammered and was raucously friendly and oozed wretchedly out of the door" (ll. 62f.)? Write a text interpretation.

13. The world depicted in Sinclair Lewis' novel is that of the post-World War I years in the United States (see l. 37: *"during the war* salesmen were hard to hire"). American trade unions did not become really influential until the New Deal legislation of President Franklin Delano Roosevelt in the 1930s. Do you think that organized labour and its principle of *collective bargaining* would make a difference in firms like Babbitt's? Write a comment.

| Style | The use of *registers* |

Analysis

14. When talking to Stanley Graff, Babbitt quickly changes the *registers* from which he chooses his words and constructions, i.e. he chooses the kind of language that is typical of distinct social roles in communication (cf. E. Werlich, *A Text Grammar of English*, Heidelberg, 1976, §§ 626f.). Which registers do you recognize? Give illustrative examples.

15. In which of these registers (see 14) does Babbitt use expressions such as these: "stuff" – "doing the lovey-dovey" – "kick about working overtime" – "a loafer"? What effects are they intended to achieve?

16. In which of the registers (see 14) does Babbitt use these expressions: "Inspiration" – "with a love for his profession" – "inspire him to do his best" – "as a matter of principle" – "unfair to the others"?
What effects are they intended to achieve?

Practice

17. What is the general impression that Babbitt's quick switch from one register to another creates of the man in the outlined situation?

18. In what way does Babbitt's final comment on his talk with Stanley Graff contribute to the reader's general impression of Babbitt:
"Today he had so passionately indulged in self-approval that he wondered whether he had been entirely just:
'After all, Stan isn't a boy any more. Oughtn't to call him so hard. But rats, got to haul folks over the coals now and then for their own good. Unpleasant duty – I wonder if Stan is sore? What's he saying to McGoun out there?'"

6. The character's speeches and actions as evidence

From: Robert Stanton, op. cit., p. 18.

The most important evidence of all is the character's own dialogue and behavior. In good fiction, every speech, every action is not only a step in the plot, but also a manifestation of character. Half the pleasure in reading a story by Henry James comes from seeing the interplay of character in the conversations. It is especially useful to go
5 through at least a few major scenes in detail, speech by speech, action by action, to determine *exactly* what is meant or implied by each of these, remembering that the characters in fiction, like real people, often misunderstand or deceive one another. Perhaps this approach seems objectionable; why not simply read the speeches and actions, instead of treating them as "evidence"? But the point is that we have not really
10 read them until we know how they exemplify character; until then, we know them only as we know the conversations of strangers we overhear on a bus. Through our knowledge of the characters, we understand their actions; through their actions, we understand the characters.

Annotations

evidence n.: (Beweismaterial) – *Henry James*: (1843–1916) great American novelist – *interplay* n.: (Zusammenspiel) – *deceive* [diˈsiːv] v.: (irreführen, täuschen) – *objectionable* [ɔbˈdʒekʃənəbl] a.: (zu beanstanden, nicht einwandfrei) – *exemplify* [igˈzemplifai] v.: (veranschaulichen, durch Beispiele erläutern) – *overhear* v.: (zufällig mit anhören).

Suggestions for discussion

1. How does Babbitt's "dialogue and behavior" *exemplify character* in his encounter with Stanley Graff?
2. How is "the interplay of character" shown in Babbitt's conversation with Graff?
3. To use Stanton's words, you have gone through a major scene "in detail, speech by speech, action by action, to determine *exactly* what is meant or implied by each of these" (ll. 5ff.). With reference to insight into character, why can one say that this approach has been "useful"? Think also of those traits of Babbitt's character which would have gone almost unnoticed in the normal reading of a novel.
4. Why, in your view, does the writer limit his observations on characters' "speeches" and "actions" to "good fiction" (l. 2)? Think of how characters are made to speak in so-called pulp fiction or popular comic strips.
5. To support his "approach", the critic repeatedly refers to the reader's knowledge of "real people" (l. 7) in concrete situations (see ll. 11f.: "the conversations of strangers we overhear on a bus"). What aspect of looking at a fictional character's way of speaking does the critic underline by showing these connections?

7. John Wain, "Got a light, mate?"

From: John Wain, *Hurry on down*. Harmondsworth, 1960, pp. 26f.

1 He gulped down the gin and immediately raised the stout to his lips. His long wait at the bar had sobered him up, and it was important to mix his drinks quickly if he wanted release.
It was not long in coming. As the long, slow gulps of stout followed the quick dash 5 of gin into his stomach, his previous drinks seemed to wake from their dormancy. One by one, the familiar signs of approaching intoxication began to assert themselves. His tongue felt slightly numb; pressed against his lower front teeth, it seemed to be covered with a sheath of flannel. The bar, as he stared down its shiny length, began to rise and fall gently. High in the ceiling, the three electric lights which glared down 10 through the clouds of smoke began to circle one another in a solemn dance.
'Got a light, mate?' came a croak from beside him. Before answering Charles raised his glass and, without hurry, poured the last third of the stout down his throat. As it foamed and splashed into the dancing ocean that awaited it, his sense of liberation became complete. When sober he would have spun round, anxious to be of service, 15 to ingratiate himself; he would have dived for his matches, probably spilling his drink as he did so. Now, he was calm, insolent, able to live on the same level as the majority of his fellows.
'Got a light?' the voice croaked again, but without resentment; thirty seconds' wait is no inconvenience. Charles carefully turned and did his best to focus on the man's 20 expanding and contracting face. Without a word he took out his matchbox, and, with extreme care, drew out the inner compartment. As it was upside down, the matches cascaded to the floor. Immediately Charles stooped to gather them up, violently thrusting against the legs of someone standing at the bar. The man staggered, protesting vehemently, but with no thought of apologizing Charles concentrated 25 doggedly on his task of collecting the matches. Whether they were in fact swimming in a puddle of spilt beer, or merely appeared to be swirling and writhing to his disordered vision, he could not tell; but it was some minutes before he had picked up the last one, and replaced them in the box with their heads all pointing the same way. Erect once more, he turned to the man who had asked for the light, and whose 30 face was no longer expanding and contracting but alternately coming close and receding to an immense distance. Again he opened the box, and selecting a match from its circling nest, struck it and held it out. But at that instant the face, which had been unbearably close to his, rushed back into the distance. With a muttered exclamation of annoyance, Charles thrust the burning match out to the full extent of his arm.
35 Immediately the face ceased to be a face, and became a purple sphere of fury with two vast coloured eyes. As the match sank sizzling into his limp moustache, and the flame flickered for an instant up his nostrils, the man started back with a hoarse cry of pain and anger. Charles, too, lurched backwards, unnerved by the sudden noise.

Since the bar was by now too full to allow of any sudden movement, elbows were
40 violently jogged, jets of beer shot out in several directions, and a loud volley of oaths
rose above the general rumble of conversation.
In his normal condition, nothing could have exceeded Charles's terror and shame in
such a situation. He had been the cause of a disturbance! He had broken the sacred
law of self-effacing, mute compliance – he had made, the phrase ran, an *exhibition of*
45 *himself!* Normally, he would not have waited, except to stammer out his apologies; the
burnt man's injured shout of 'It's 'is fault! Throw the clumsy bastard out! Had too
much he has!' would have found him halfway to the door. But now the healing mist
of alcohol, half gentle detachment and half fierce arrogance, protected him even
against the menacing approach of the landlord. Instead of quailing before the
50 hailstorm of abuse that swept at him from behind the bar, he merely blinked benignly
for a moment at the landlord's whirling face – now dominated by the out-thrust
nose, now grotesquely receding under the overhanging eyebrows – and then, turning
coolly on his heel, calmly opened the door and went out, to be greeted by the warm
silence of the summer night, and the village street opening and closing like a huge
55 oyster shell.

I. Notes on the text

The text is an unabridged passage from John Wain's novel *Hurry on down* (first
published in 1953). The novel is about a young graduate's unconventional search
for his place in society.
John Wain (b. 1925) belongs among those post-war British novelists who use a
precise contemporary language in rendering their view of life. Like the novels and
narratives of Kingsley Amis (for instance, *Lucky Jim*), John Braine (for instance,
Room at the top and *Life at the top*), and Allan Sillitoe (for instance, *The Loneliness
of the Long-Distance Runner*), those of John Wain tend to present heroes who
strongly reject the conventions and values of the society into which they were born.

II. Words

got past part.: elliptic for *have you got* – *light* n.: means of making a fire, match –
gulp s.th. down v.: take large mouthfuls of (einen großen Zug, Schluck nehmen) –
stout n.: strong dark beer – *sober up* v.: become less drunk – *release* n.: state of being
set free from duties, pain, etc. – *dormancy* n.: state of inactivity (Schlaf-, Ruhe-
zustand) – *intoxication* n.: state of being drunk (Trunkenheit, Rausch) – *assert
oneself* v.: push oneself forward aggressively (sich geltend machen) – *numb* [nʌm] a.:
without feeling – *sheath* n.: (here:) covering layer (Hülle, Futteral) – *flannel* n.:
loosely woven woollen material – *glare* v.: give out a dazzling light (grell leuchten) –
croak n.: hoarse sound – *foam* v.: produce a mass of small bubbles on a surface of
liquid (schäumen) – *splash* v.: cause (liquid) to scatter in jets (Strahlen) or drops –
sober a.: not drunk (nüchtern) – *spin round* v.: turn rapidly round – *anxious to* a.:
eager, very desirous to – *ingratiate oneself with s.o.:* make oneself agreeable to, try
to win favour from (sich bei jmdm. lieb Kind machen) – *dive* v.: plunge one's hand

25

into – *spill* v.: let (liquid) fall from a vessel (Gefäß) (verschütten) – *insolent* [ˈinsəulənt] a.: rude, insulting (unverschämt) – *resentment* n.: act of regarding as an insult; anger at an insult (Unmut, Groll) – *inconvenience* [.inkənˈviːnjəns] n.: cause of discomfort (Unannehmlichkeit) – *focus on* v.: concentrate on – *cascade* [-ˈ-] v.: fall in rich streams like a waterfall – *stoop* v.: curve the head and upper body forwards and down (sich bücken) – *stagger* v.: stand or walk unsteadily – *apologize* [əˈpɔlədʒaiz] v.: express regret (for a fault) – *dogged* [ˈdɔgid] a.: unreasonably determined (verbissen) – *swirl* v.: move fast in a circle (herumwirbeln) – *writhe* [ˈraið] v.: twist the body as if suffering pain – *alternately* adv.: first one then the other (abwechselnd) – *recede* [riˈsiːd] v.: move backwards – *sizzle* v.: make a hissing noise (zischen) – *limp* a.: lacking stiffness, soft (schlaff) – *moustache* [məsˈtaːʃ] n.: hair on upper lip – *nostrils* n.: the two openings of the nose – *lurch* v.: move in unsteady jerks (taumeln) – *jog* v.: push gently – *jet* n.: stream of liquid forced from a small opening under pressure (Strahl) – *volley* n.: (here:) rapid series of aggressive words or acts – *oaths* n.: (here:) blasphemous curses or exclamations – *rumble* n.: low, continuous, rolling sound – *exceed* v.: go beyond – *disturbance* n.: act of breaking up the quiet of, disorder, tumult – *self-effacing* a.: avoiding being noticed, being willing to give first place to others (sich selbst verleugnend) – *mute* a.: silent, speechless (stumm) – *compliance* [kəmˈplaiəns] n.: disposition to give in to others (Willfährigkeit) – *clumsy* a.: inelegant in movements – *bastard* [ˈbaːstəd] n.: (vulgar usage) unpleasant or ill-tempered person – *detachment* n.: disinterestedness (Gleichgültigkeit, Abstand) – *fierce* a.: unrestrained, violent – *menacing* [ˈmenəsiŋ] a.: threatening (drohend) – *quail* v.: be afraid (verzagen, den Mut verlieren) – *abuse* [əˈbjuːs] n.: (here:) grossly insulting language (Beschimpfung) – *blink* v.: move the eyelids quickly up and down – *benign* [biˈnain] a.: kindly, gracious (gütig).

III. Key terms for detailed field study of words (semantic fields, collocations)

The following terms may be used in order to group systematically the most important word material of the text for more efficient word learning:

1. *characterization of persons*: drinking

2. *characterization of persons*: bodily gestures and movements

IV. Suggestions for guided analysis and practice

| Content | The place |

Analysis

1. Where are the related events set? Collect references to the place from the text and explain what it is like.

2. What situation does the writer depict in this place? Try to sum up the situation in one or two sentences.

Practice

3. What connection between inside and outside the place does the writer suggest when, at the end, presenting his protagonist ([prəuˈtægənist] – Hauptheld) Charles as walking out, being "greeted by the warm silence of the summer night, and the village street opening and closing like a huge oyster shell" (ll. 53ff.)? Write a short explanatory comment.

| Content | The people in the place

Analysis

4. Which would you consider the most telling reference to the kind of people to be found in the place?

Practice

5. What conclusions about the people in the place can you draw from the first of these references (see 4)?
6. Which other references in the text can be adduced (anführen) to support your view above (see 5)? Write an explanatory comment on the references you quote.

| Content | The protagonist

Analysis

7. Where in the text is the protagonist's state of "approaching intoxication" most clearly reflected?
8. What effect on the protagonist has his being confronted with the request for a light in this condition?

Practice

9. What view of his behaviour does Charles reveal when thinking in the following terms:
". . . his sense of liberation became complete. When sober he would have spun round, anxious to be of service, to ingratiate himself [. . .]. Now, he was calm, insolent, able to live on the same level as the majority of his fellows" (ll. 13ff.)? Write a short comment.

10. What conclusions about the protagonist's social position can you draw from his following reflections:
"He had been the cause of a disturbance! He had broken the sacred law of self-effacing, mute compliance – he had made, the phrase ran, an *exhibition of himself*" (ll. 43ff.)? Write a short text interpretation.

11. What is your view of the new position that the protagonist takes in the course of the outlined events (see 9 and 10)? Discuss his position in a comment.

| Composition | Climactic structuring[1]

Analysis

12. The narration of the incident with the light is structured so as to produce a major climax. Which sentence would you consider as presenting the major climax in the story above?

Practice

13. Which aspects mark this sentence (see 12) as a climax in this text? Think of both its form and its content.

| Composition |

Analysis

14. There is another minor climax in the story before this major one. With which sentence would you associate it?

Practice

15. Compare the two climaxes in the story and explain in what they differ.

| Text type |

Analysis

16. In telling his story, John Wain makes use of different points of view in order to present a lively *narrative*. Which difference in *point of view* do you recognize in sentences such as the following:
(1) "Without a word he took out his matchbox, and, with extreme care, drew out the inner compartment. As it was upside down, the matches cascaded to the floor" (ll. 20ff.);

---

[1] For a general introduction to *climactic structuring* in narratives, see E. Werlich, *Text Analysis and Text Production*. Book 1: *Stories and Reports*. Dortmund, 1975, §§ 7.1 and 9.

(2) "He had been the cause of a disturbance! He had broken the sacred law of self-effacing, mute compliance – he had made, the phrase ran, an *exhibition of himself!*" (ll. 43ff.)?

Practice

17. What is the established technical term of literary criticism for the second of the described points of view (see 16)? Consult your dictionary for text analysis under key terms such as *language in a novel*.

8. The treatment of point of view in a story

From: Robert Stanton, op. cit., pp. 27f.

1 The treatment of point of view in a story is guided by two main purposes. As we know, serious fiction should enable us to imagine and understand a human experience. Authors today, like most of us, are intensely aware that every man's experience is shaped and colored by his insight, temperament, background, and prejudices – in
5 other words, by his point of view. If, therefore, we are to imagine a character's experience, we must share his point of view. But if we are also to *understand* his experience, we must understand his point of view; and understanding is different from sharing. We must understand the character himself, and consciously recognize everything that colors his view of things. In a film, if a character is abnormally afraid of
10 rats, the camera can show us a close-up of a rat as he sees it, vicious and filthy. But it can also show us the character's perspiring face and terrified eyes, and thus make us conscious of the abnormality of his fear. We have, in other words, *two* points of view, the character's and the camera's: we share the first, but we understand it by means of the second.
15 In a story, the author is the "camera." Usually, his view of the characters appears through his technique, his tone, his literary devices, rather than through explicit comments; but it is always present, and we accept it as our own – at least while reading the story – just as we accept the camera's eyes as our own. Like the camera, the author can bring us into a character's point of view so that we share his experience; but
20 also like the camera, the author must be able to remove us from the character so that we can contemplate and understand him – even though the story is told in the character's words. We must both share the illusion of experience and stand outside the illusion. If we simply identify ourselves with the character, the result is not literature but a synthetic daydream.

Annotations

intensely adv.: (äußerst, höchst) – *vicious* a.: (bösartig) – *filthy* a.: (dreckig) – *perspire* v.: (schwitzen) – *remove* v.: (entfernen) – *contemplate* ['---] v.: (betrachten).

Suggestions for discussion

1. What narrative technique does John Wain use in "'Got a light, mate?'" to make the reader "imagine" the "character's experience" (ll. 5f.)?
2. Which of the two points of view that Stanton distinguishes (see ll. 12f.) is represented in this sentence from Wain's narrative: "The bar, as he stared down its shiny length, began to rise and fall gently"; ll. 8f.)?
3. Apart from the sentence quoted under question 16 above, where else do you find instances of "the camera's" point of view, which is "the author's"?
4. Against the background of both Wain's short narrative and Stanton's text, how would you explain the last sentence, "If we simply identify ourselves with the character, the result is not literature but a synthetic daydream" (ll. 23f.)?
5. In his introductory sentence, the critic claims that "*serious fiction* should enable us to imagine and understand a human experience" (l. 2). Which of these two aspects is absent from the fiction of mass-produced magazines?

9. The first-person singular point of view in fictional texts

From: E. Werlich, *A Text Grammar of English*. Heidelberg, 1976; pp. 135f.

1   In fictional text form variants such as the *poem, short story* or *novel*, the first-person *I* is not to be identified directly with the actual encoder, i.e. the poet or author. It is a fictional *I* which represents a *cotextually* more specifically determined *role* or *mask*. In fictional texts, the role of the first-person *I* may be explicitly labelled (as in most
5   stories) or only implied (as in most *poems*); the role may be that of a fictitious omniscient speaker (narrator) who can comment on all events and speak from inside characters (as in certain kinds of *novel*), or the much more limited role of one of the fictional characters (as in single-character narration).
    In Shakespeare's *Sonnet 18* ("Shall *I* compare thee to a Summer's day?"), the role of the
10 speaker is cotextually determined both as a *lover* praising a beautiful woman and as a *poet* praising Muse [...]. The narrator in Hemingway's short story "Old Man at the Bridge" (see, for example, "It was *my* task to cross the bridge, explore the bridgehead beyond and find out to what point the enemy had advanced. *I* did this and returned ...") is cotextually delimited as an *officer* in the Spanish Civil War.

Annotations

cotextual a.: (den umgebenden Text betreffend, kotextuell) – *label* [ˈleibəl] v.:
(benennen, bezeichnen) – *fictitious* a.: (frei erfunden, fiktiv) – *omniscient* [ɔmˈnisiənt]
a.: (allwissend) – *delimit* [-ˈ--] v.: (eingrenzen).

Suggestions for discussion

1. What "*cotextually* more specifically determined *role*" do you find in John Wain's text?
2. Narration from a first-person singular point of view imposes certain limits upon the author. What changes would the first-person singular point of view necessitate, for instance, in John Wain's short narrative?

10. Lawrence Durrell, The change a uniform makes

From: Lawrence Durrell, *Mountolive*. London, 1958, pp. 131–133.

1 It was frightfully hot in the little cabin of the airplane. Mountolive wrestled in a desultory tormented fashion with his uniform. Skinners had done wonders with it – it fitted like a glove; but the *weight* of it. It was like being dressed in a boxing-glove. He would be parboiled. He felt the sweat pouring down his chest, tickling him.
5 His mixed elation and alarm translated itself into queasiness. Was he going to be airsick – and for the first time in his life? He hoped not. It would be awful to be sick into this impressive refurbished hat. "Five minutes to touchdown"; words scribbled on a page torn from an operations pad. Good. Good. He nodded mechanically and found himself fanning his face with this musical-comedy object.
10 At any rate, it became him. He was quite surprised to see how handsome he looked in a mirror.

They circled softly down and the mauve dusk rose to meet them. It was as if the whole of Egypt were settling softly into an inkwell. Then flowering out of the golden whirls sent up by stray dust-devils he glimpsed the nippled minarets and towers of the
15 famous tombs; the Moquattam hills were pink and nacreous as a finger-nail.

On the airfield were grouped the dignitaries who had been detailed to receive him officially. They were flanked by the members of his own staff with their wives – all wearing garden-party hats and gloves as if they were in the paddock at Longchamps. Everyone was nevertheless perspiring freely, indeed in streams. Mountolive felt *terra firma* under his polished dress shoes and drew a sigh of relief. The ground was almost hotter than the plane; but his nausea had vanished. He stepped forward tentatively to shake hands and realized that with the donning of his uniform everything had changed. A sudden loneliness smote him – for he realized that now, as an Ambassador, he must forever renounce the friendship of ordinary human beings in exchange for their *deference*. His uniform encased him like a suit of chain-armour. It shut him off from the ordinary world of human exchanges. "God!" he thought, "I shall be forever soliciting a normal human reaction from people who are bound to defer to my *rank!* I shall become like that dreadful parson in Sussex who always feebly swears in order to prove that he is really quite an ordinary human being despite the dog-collar!" But the momentary spasm of loneliness passed in the joys of a new self-possession. There was nothing to do now but to exploit his charm to the full; to be handsome, to be capable, surely one had the right to enjoy the consciousness of these things without self-reproach? He proved himself upon the outer circle of Egyptian officials whom he greeted in excellent Arabic. Smiles broke out everywhere, at once merging into a confluence of self-congratulatory looks. He knew also how to present himself in half-profile to the sudden stare of flashbulbs as he made his first speech – a tissue of heart-warming platitudes pronounced with charming diffidence in Arabic which won murmurs of delight and excitement from the raffish circle of journalists.

A band suddenly struck up raggedly, playing woefully out of key; and under the plaintive iterations of a European melody played somehow in quartertones he recognized his own National Anthem. It was startling, and he had difficulty in not smiling. The police mission had been diligently training the Egyptian force in the uses of the slide-trombone. But the whole performance had a desultory and impromptu air, as if some rare form of ancient music (Palestrina) were being interpreted on a set of fire-irons. He stood stiffly to attention. An aged Bimbashi with a glass eye stood before the band, also at attention – albeit rather shakily. Then it was over. "I'm sorry about the band," said Nimrod Pasha under his breath. "You see, sir, it was a scratch team. Most of the musicians are ill." Mountolive nodded gravely, sympathetically, and addressed himself to the next task. He walked with profuse keenness up and down a guard of honour to inspect their bearing; the men smelt strongly of sesame oil and sweat and one or two smiled affably. This was delightful. He restrained the impulse to grin back. Then, turning, he completed his devoirs to the Protocol section, warm and smelly too in its brilliant red flower-pot hats. Here the smiles rolled about, scattered all over the place like slices of unripe water-melon. An Ambassador who spoke Arabic! He put on the air of smiling diffidence which he knew best charmed. He had learned this. His crooked smile was appealing – even his own staff was visibly much taken with him, he noted with pride; but particularly the wives. They relaxed and turned their faces towards him like flower-traps. He had a few words for each of the secretaries.

Then at last the great car bore him smoothly away to the Residence on the banks of the Nile.

I. Notes on the text

The text is an unabridged passage from Durrell's novel *Mountolive* (1958), the third part of his tetralogy *The Alexandria Quartet* (1962). The first three volumes tell of a series of events in Alexandria, Egypt, before the Second World War; the fourth is set in the war years.

Lawrence Durrell was born in Darjeeling, India, in 1912 and spent most of his life outside England. He was press attaché to the British embassies in Cairo and Alexandria during the Second World War. Later, his career in the diplomatic service took him to the Greek islands, Yugoslavia and Cyprus.

II. Words

wrestle with v.: struggle with – *desultory* [ˈdesəltəri] a.: unmethodical (planlos) – *torment* [tɔːˈment] v.: cause extreme pain to – *glove* [glʌv] n.: covering for a hand, especially one with a separate compartment for each finger (Handschuh) – *parboil* v.: boil partially (halb kochen, ankochen) – *tickle* v.: (kitzeln) – *elation* n.: proud delight (gehobene Stimmung) – *queasiness* n.: state of feeling sick (Übelkeit) – *refurbish* v.: polish up again – *touchdown* n.: first contact of aircraft with ground on landing – *operations pad* n.: number of sheets of writing paper fastened together as used by the military – *fan* v.: blow gently – *become s.o.* v.: look well on s.o. – *mauve* [məuv] a.: bright but delicate pale purple (malvenfarbig) – *inkwell* n.: cup for holding ink which fits into a hole in a desk – *whirl* n.: rapid rotation (Wirbel) – *stray* a.: seen or happening occasionally (vereinzelt) – *dust-devil* n.: whirling pillar of sand, only a few yards broad but up to 3,000 ft high, moving forward at up to 30 m.p.h. – *nippled* a.: looking like the teat of a woman's breast – *tomb* [tuːm] n.: grave with a monument over it – *pink* a.: pale red, rosy – *nacreous* [ˈneikriəs] a.: (perlmutterartig) – *dignitary* [ˈdignitəri] n.: person holding high office – *detail* [ˈdiːteil] v.: appoint for special duty (abkommandieren) – *paddock* n.: enclosure where racehorses are assembled before a race – *Longchamps*: racecourse in Paris – *perspire* [pəːˈspaiə] v.: produce moisture (Feuchtigkeit) through skin pores, sweat – *dress shoes* n.: shoes for formal wear – *nausea* [ˈnɔːsiə] n.: feeling of sickness (Übelkeit) – *tentative* a.: (versuchend) – *don* v.: put on (a garment) – *smote* [sməut] v.: past tense of *smite*: strike powerfully – *renounce* v.: give up; withdraw from – *deference* [ˈdefərəns] n.: respect (Ehrerbietung) – *encase* v.: surround or cover as with a case, enclose completely (umhüllen, einschließen) – *chain-armour* n.: (Kettenpanzer [Rüstung]) – *solicit* [səˈlisit] v.: request earnestly and persistently – *bound* a.: compelled, obliged – *defer to* v.: submit to another's wish or judgement – *parson* n.: clergyman – *feeble* a.: weak, infirm – *dog-collar* n.: (coll.) clergyman's collar fastening at the back – *spasm* n.: strong, but short-lived burst – *self-possession* n.: self-confidence – *self-reproach* n.: disapproval of one's own actions, attitudes, etc. – *Arabic* [ˈærəbik] n.: the language spoken by Arabs – *merge into* v.: become completely absorbed into – *confluence* n.: a flowing together – *self-congratulatory* a.: expressing one's joy to oneself on one's success – *flashbulb* n.: lamp used in taking photographs in darkness or dim light – *tissue* [ˈtiʃuː] n.: fine fabric; web – *platitude* n.: dull and trite remark – *diffidence* n.: shyness – *raffish* a.:

disreputable – *ragged* ['rægid] a.: (here:) with the musicians not all starting at the same time – *woeful* ['wəufəl] a.: full of misery – *plaintive* a.: mournful; grieving – *iteration* n.: that which is repeated – *the National Anthem* ['ænθəm] n.: song used by any country as a symbol of its national identity – *slide-trombone* n.: (Zugposaune) – *impromptu* [im'prɔmptju:] a.: without preparation, improvised – *Palestrina*: Italian composer (1525–1594), a master of contrapuntal composition – *fire-irons* n.: instruments used for stirring a domestic fire – *albeit* [ɔːl'biːt] conj.: even though, although – *scratch* a.: gathered hastily from various sources; of uneven standard – *profuse* [prəu'fjuːs] a.: excessive – *keenness* n.: eagerness – *bearing* ['bɛəriŋ] n.: (Haltung) – *sesame* ['sesəmi] n.: East Indian plant with oily edible seeds – *affable* ['æfəbl] a.: courteous – *devoirs* [də'vwɑːz] n.: courteous attentions to – *protocol* ['prəutəukɔl] n.: rules of diplomatic etiquette or procedure – *crooked* ['krukid] a.: dishonest – *be much taken with s.o.*: respond positively to s.o. – *flower-trap* n.: flower that turns its face towards the sun – *smooth* [smuːð] a.: moving easily and evenly – *the Residence*: (here:) big house where a foreign diplomat lives.

III. Key terms for detailed field study of words (semantic fields, collocations)

The following terms may be used in order to group systematically the most important word material of the text for more efficient word learning:

1. *transport*: by air
2. *society*: rituals (the official reception)
3. *man*: clothes
4. *man*: sensation

IV. Suggestions for guided analysis and practice

| Content | The situation |

Analysis

1. What situation does the text deal with? State in one or two summarizing sentences.
2. What role has Mountolive, the protagonist, in this situation?
3. Which features of the situation, from the contemporary point of view, are unusual, considering the protagonist's role?

Practice

4. How can these features (see 3) be explained from a historical point of view? Think of Britain and Egypt in the first half of the 20th century.

5. Despite its historical setting, the analysed situation has features which can still be observed as elements of a contemporary ceremony or 'ritual'. Which features are these?

> **Content**   The protagonist

Analysis

6. From what point of view does Lawrence Durrell present the protagonist in the outlined situation? Take into consideration sentences such as, "He felt the sweat pouring down his chest, tickling him. His mixed elation and alarm translated itself into queasiness. Was he going to be airsick – and for the first time in his life?" (ll. 4ff.)
7. What effect does this presentation of the protagonist create with reference to the other people mentioned in the text?
8. Why can this presentation of the protagonist and the other people (see 6–7) be considered very unusual in the outlined situation type (see 1–5)?
9. What may the reader be struck by when he compares the protagonist's outward behaviour with his train of thought?

Practice

10. What is the effect of the reader being confronted, for instance, with sentences about the protagonist such as these: "Mountolive wrestled in a desultory tormented fashion with his uniform . . . it fitted like a glove; but the *weight* of it. It was like being dressed in a boxing-glove" (ll. 1–4); and, "Was he going to be airsick – and for the first time in his life? He hoped not. It would be awful to be sick into this impressive refurbished hat" (ll. 5–7)?

> **Content**   The protagonist's role

Analysis

11. What experience does the protagonist undergo in the situation?
12. What importance does his "uniform" assume in this connection?

Practice

13. What impression, do you think, is the whole text intended to create about the historical situation? Take into consideration your answers under 10–12.

> **Composition**

Analysis

14. The text opens with an important reference to space: "in the little cabin of the airplane". How is this opening reference continued in the text?
15. What order do these spatial references establish in the text?

Practice

16. There are also a number of spatial references in the text which show the protagonist "encased" by things or people. Can you list some of these?
17. One might say that all these spatial references (see 16) symbolically point to the protagonist's new situation. Could you explain why one might say this?

11. Aspects of the setting of a story

From: Harry Fenson/Hildreth Kritzer, *Reading, Understanding, and Writing about Short Stories*. New York, 1966, pp. 30f.

One element of fiction which even the most inexperienced reader is likely to be conscious of is *setting* – the physical background against which the events of a story or novel work themselves out. Children with very little interest in or consciousness of fiction as a comment on human nature and experience will often choose their reading on the basis of their interest in a particular setting – jungle life, the mountains of the moon or the swamps of Venus, or, less exotically, stories about life in an exclusive boarding school or the dugouts of baseball teams or the pits of the hot-rodders. For the child, such stories serve the purpose of taking him out of the confines of his own home, neighborhood, and shopping center and bringing him into a larger, more interesting world, a world created largely by the verisimilitude of the descriptive details of setting.
Much of this same primitive interest in the verisimilitude of the details of setting persists as our reading becomes more mature in interest and appreciation. Even in complex and sophisticated stories, a vividly depicted setting which creates an illusion of reality carries its own interest and helps us accept more readily and sympathetically the existence of the fictional world, the inhabitants of that world, and their behaviour. But as we learn to consider the story as a dramatically unified representation of, and significant comment upon, human nature, the element of setting comes to assume a fuller importance and interest for us. We begin to see setting as one of the elements contributing to the total unity of the story, its details chosen not merely because they are "realistic" or interesting in themselves but because they contribute significantly to the working out of the theme. We find that details of time and place; of physical, social, and intellectual milieus; of emotional atmosphere are not merely "description"; they are functional. They help unfold action and conflict, contribute to our understanding of the characters and their motivation, and illuminate the emotional significance of the story by helping to create atmosphere and tone. [...]
The details of setting in stories vary in scope and quantity. The author may limit his action to as small an area as a room or a street, or he may use a background rich with descriptions of physical nature, landscape, topography, and climate. [...]

30 The author may concentrate his description of setting in the exposition of the story or, more commonly, he may spread the details throughout the narrative. But always the details are selective, part of the total economy of the story, and generally they serve more than one purpose.

Annotations

swamps [swɔmps] n.: (Sümpfe) – *dugout* n.: (Unterstand, Bunker) – *pit* n.: (Box neben einer Rennbahnstrecke) – *hot-rodder* n.: (Fahrer eines Autos mit frisiertem Motor, jugendlicher Rennfahrer) – *confines* [ˈ---] n.: (Grenzen, Begrenzung) – *verisimilitude* [ˌverisiˈmilitjuːd] n.: (Wahrscheinlichkeit) – *persist* [pəˈsist] v.: (andauern) – *mature* [məˈtjuə] a.: (reif) – *sophisticated* [səˈfistikeitid] a.: (intellektuell hochentwickelt) – *illuminate* v.: (erhellen, beleuchten) – *scope* n.: (Umfang, Reichweite) – *topography* [tɔˈpɔgrəfi] n.: ([Beschreibung der] Geländeoberfläche) – *economy* n.: ([An]Ordnung, Bau).

Suggestions for discussion

1. Durrell's narrative fits the critics' observation that stories with a memorable setting transport the reader "into a larger and more interesting world" (ll. 9f.). Why?
2. Illustrate by Durrell's narrative details of setting, such as "details of time and place; of physical, social, and intellectual milieus; of emotional atmosphere" (ll. 22f.).
3. Against your knowledge of Durrell's narrative, how would you explain the critics' observation that the "details of setting" are "functional" (l. 24), that "they serve more than one purpose" (l. 32)?

12. Clues to symbolism in a story

From: M. H. Abrams, *A Glossary of Literary Terms*. New York, 1971 (3rd edition), pp. 168–169.

1 A symbol, in the broadest sense of the term, is anything which signifies something else; in this sense all words are symbols. As commonly used in discussing literature, however, symbol is applied only to a word or set of words that signifies an object or event which itself signifies something else; that is, the words refer to something which
5 suggests a range of reference beyond itself. Some symbols are "conventional" or "public"; thus "the Cross," "the Red, White, and Blue," "the Good Shepherd" are terms that signify symbolic objects of which the further significance is fixed and

37

traditional in a particular culture. Poets, like all of us, use such conventional symbols; many poets, however, also use "private" or "personal symbols," which they develop
10 themselves. Often they do so by exploiting preexisting and widely shared associations with an object or action – for example, the general tendency to associate a peacock with pride and an eagle with heroic endeavor, or to associate the rising sun with birth and the setting sun with death, or to associate climbing with effort or progress and descent with surrender or failure. Some poets, however, often use symbols whose significance
15 they mainly generate for themselves, and these set the reader a more difficult problem in interpretation.

Annotations

signify [ˑ---] v.: (bezeichnen, bedeuten) – *range of reference* n.: (Bezugsbereich) – *shepherd* [ˑʃepəd] n.: (Hirte, Schäfer) – *exploit* v.: (nutzen, ausnutzen) – *preexist* v.: (bereits existieren, vorgegeben sein) – *peacock* n.: (Pfau) – *eagle* n.: (Adler) – *endeavor* [inˑdevə] n.: (B.E. *endeavour*: Unternehmungsgeist) – *descent* [diˑsent] n.: (Abstieg) – *surrender* [səˑrendə] n.: (Aufgabe, Niederlage) – *generate* v.: (erzeugen, hervorbringen).

Suggestions for discussion

1. Which "'conventional' or 'public'" symbols do you find in Durrell's text?
2. In what way does Durrell change this symbol (see 1) into a "'private' or 'personal symbol'" (l. 9)?

13. Kinds of symbols

From: Harry Fenson/Hildreth Kritzer, op. cit., pp. 57f.

1 The very nature of symbolism, *suggesting something other than (conceptual), but related to, that which is stated or presented (tangible)*, admittedly involves an explanation that is far from simple. Nevertheless, it may be possible to develop a useful, if limited, understanding of symbolism rather than one that explores all the
5 psychological and rhetorical complexities that constitute the broadest definition of the symbolic process. There are basically two kinds of symbols employed in fiction, the *established* and the *created* symbol.

Established Symbols

An established symbol is one which utilizes a tangible-conceptual relationship which has already been established in the reader's mind because it has been used long and often throughout our literary and religious heritage. The most obvious examples are the cross, suggesting Christianity; the rose, suggesting love; and the color white, suggesting purity. A less obvious but nonetheless established symbol is derived from an *allusion,* a specific reference to a name or lines from the Bible or a wellknown work of literature. Faulkner's title *The Sound and the Fury* is taken from these lines in *Macbeth:*

> It is a tale
> Told by an idiot, full of sound and fury,
> Signifying nothing.

suggesting a nihilistic approach to life.

Created Symbols

A created symbol is one which causes a tangible-conceptual relationship to be suggested to the reader's mind because of its recurrence in similar contexts, or because of its juxtaposition to a particular character or event in the story. This is probably the most difficult kind of symbol to identify because its suggestive characteristic depends on the reader's ability to discriminate between what is purposive and what is incidental. A descriptive passage, for example, may in its concrete detail serve to add realism to a story by rooting it in a setting that is vividly [evocative] of a specific time and place; on the other hand, the choice of detail may serve to suggest something about the setting that transcends the tangible details themselves.

Annotations

conceptual a.: (dem Vorstellungsbereich angehörend, begrifflich) – *tangible* a.: (greif-, berührbar) – *admittedly* adv.: (zugegebenermaßen) – *involve* v.: (nach sich ziehen) – *established* a.: (hier: vorgegeben, etabliert) – *utilize* [ˈjuːtilaiz] v.: (nutzen, ausschöpfen) – *heritage* [ˈheritidʒ] n.: (Erbe) – *purity* n.: (Reinheit) – *allusion* n.: (Anspielung) – *recurrence* [riˈkʌrəns] n.: (Wiederkehr) – *juxtaposition* [ˌdʒʌkstəpəˈziʃən] n.: (Nebeneinanderstellung) – *discriminate between* v.: (unterscheiden zwischen) – *purposive* a.: (absichtsvoll) – *incidental* a.: (zufällig) – *root s.th.* v.: (verwurzeln) – *transcend* [trænˈsend] v.: (überschreiten, hinausgehen über).

Suggestions for discussion

1. In Durrell's narrative, how do the spatial references which show the protagonist encased by things or people suggest something "conceptual" that is related to what is "stated or presented (tangible)"? Consider your analysis above (questions 16 and 17).

2. Both an "established" and a "created symbol" may be recognized in this sentence from Durrell's narrative: "His uniform encased him like a suit of chain-armour" (l. 25). Which are they?

14. Plot, the backbone of a story

From: Robert Stanton, *An Introduction to Fiction*. New York, 1965, pp. 15f.

The plot is the backbone of a story. Because it is more self-evident than some of the story's other elements, we may say little about it in analysis; but without a clear knowledge of its events, its links of cause-and-effect, its degree of inevitability, we cannot hope to understand the story further. Like all other elements of a story, the plot has its own laws: it must have a true beginning, middle, and end; it must be plausible and logical, and yet it should occasionally surprise us; it must arouse and satisfy suspense.

The movement of a plot comes chiefly from its ability to arouse questions in our minds, appealing to our curiosity, hope, and fear. The simplest question is "What happens next?" But often the questions are more specific than this, and their answers may be delayed for many pages. Dickens' *A Christmas Carol* begins with a violent conflict between Scrooge's meanness and the friendly cheer of Christmas (personified by Scrooge's nephew, his poor clerk, and the charity solicitors). We hope to see Scrooge punished and the Christmas spirit triumphant at the end. Yet if Scrooge suffers, will not the Christmas spirit be violated? How can both our hopes be satisfied? This is the story's main question, not to be answered until the end. After Scrooge reaches his home, the ominous atmosphere hints at an approaching terror: what will it be? Marley's ghost answers this question and provides another, by announcing three more ghosts to come. What will they be like? When the Ghost of Christmas Past has made its visit, we wonder what the other ghosts will reveal – and so on, through literally dozens of questions. Finally, Scrooge recognizes the meanness and emptiness of his life and becomes a kindly old philanthropist. Our main question has been answered, the suspense ends, and the story is over. A skillful author uses such questions to sharpen and control our attention. When a story seems dull and formless – when we complain that "nothing happens" – the reason may be that we have missed or misunderstood these questions, and so our attention is in the wrong place.

The most effective questions are those that seem impossible to answer satisfactorily. Although we want the hero to succeed, we see that the odds against him are insuperable; although we want the villain imprisoned, we realize that this will cause his wife and children to suffer. The more conscious we are of these difficulties, the more unexpected and satisfying a convincing solution will seem. In *Moby-Dick*, we are told that Captain Ahab is hunting the white whale, Moby Dick, to avenge the loss of his leg. As the hunt proceeds, we learn that Ahab's monomaniacal desire for revenge has given him tremendous force of personality, capable of welding his crew together into a single weapon. We learn, too, that Moby Dick is one of the great forces of nature – almost, indeed, supernatural. Gradually we realize that this conflict is between two irresistible forces. But in such a conflict, which antagonist can triumph? What satisfactory ending can the conflict have?

The answer is that *neither* antagonist triumphs. Moby Dick escapes, and Ahab is strangled by a loop of his own line as he hurls the harpoon at the whale. This outcome is unexpected, and yet exactly right. We know by this point in the novel that Ahab's suffering has been caused more by his own obsession with revenge than by the whale. What can be more appropriate than to have Ahab's death caused by his own final revengeful act? Thus the outcome, as in most effective stories, is unexpected and yet appropriate, surprising and yet plausible. E. M. Forster says in *Aspects of the Novel* that a "shock, followed by the feeling, 'Oh, that's all right,' is a sign that all is well with the plot." This does not mean that a story should have a "surprise ending." A surprise ending amuses us because it is bizarre but possible, a sort of practical joke upon the reader. But the joke is ruined after the first reading. When, on the other hand, and outcome is unexpected because it convincingly answers a difficult plot-question, we can enjoy its unexpectedness again and again, as often as we reread the story.

Two important elements of plot are *conflict* and *climax*. Every work of fiction contains obvious *internal conflicts* between two desires within a character, or *external conflicts* between characters or between a character and his environment. These specific conflicts are in turn subordinate to the *central conflict,* which may be internal, external, or both. In *Huckleberry Finn,* Huck is in conflict with his father, with the Duke and the Dauphin, and with several other characters; he continually argues with himself about helping Jim to escape; he often opposes what society approves. But all these conflicts reduce to the central conflict between Huck's essential goodness and honesty, and the cruelty and hypocrisy of the world around him. As this example illustrates, a central conflict is always between fundamental and contrasting *qualities* or *forces,* such as honesty and hypocrisy, innocence and experience, individuality and the pressure conform. This conflict is the core of the story's structure, the generating center out of which the plot grows. A story may contain more than one conflict of forces, but only the central conflict fully accounts for the events of the plot. Obviously, the central conflict of a story is intimately related to its theme: the two may even be identical. (Students often misapply the term "conflict" to any vaguely defined turmoil in a story or to merely contrasting forces. The term applies properly only to a pair of forces each of which is attempting to conquer the other or resisting being conquered by it.)

The *climax* of the story is the moment at which the conflict is most intense and at which its outcome becomes inevitable. In *Moby-Dick,* the climax is Ahab's death. The climax of a story is the meeting point of its lines of force and determines how their opposition will be resolved — "resolved" rather than "decided," because although one force may vanquish the other, more often, as in real life, the outcome is a complex equilibrium in which neither side completely triumphs or completely loses. Sometimes the main climax is not a spectacular event, and sometimes it is hard to identify because the subordinate conflicts may have their own climaxes. In fact, if the central conflict of a novel appears in several forms or passes through several distinct stages, it may be impossible to fix on *one* main climax. But looking for one is always worth the effort; even the search illuminates the structure of a story.

I. Notes on the text

The text is from a book on "the principal elements, techniques, and types of fiction" (Preface). Besides *plot*, Stanton examines *character*, *theme*, and *setting* as basic elements of fiction. At the time of publication, Robert Stanton taught at the University of Washington.

II. Words

backbone n.: line of bones down the middle of the back; (here:) chief support – *self-evident* a.: clear without proof – *inevitability* n.: what is sure to happen, what cannot be avoided (Unausweichlichkeit) – *arouse* [əˈrauz] v.: excite, stir up – *suspense* [səsˈpens] n.: uncertainty (about events, decisions, etc.) (Spannung) – *curiosity* [kjuəriˈɔsiti] n.: state of being eager to know (Neugierde) – *A Christmas Carol*: a Christmas book by Charles Dickens, published in 1843. "Scrooge, an old curmudgeon [Geizhals, Griesgram], receives on Christmas Eve a visit from the ghost of Marley, his late partner in business, and beholds a series of visions of the past, present, and future, including one of what his own death will be like unless he is quick to amend his ways. As a result of this he wakes up on Christmas morning an altered man. He sends a turkey to his ill-used clerk, Bob Cratchit, positively enjoys subscribing to Christmas charities, and generally behaves like the genial old fellow that he has become" (cf. *The Oxford Companion to English Literature*, 3rd ed., p. 160). – *meanness* n.: (of behaviour) unworthiness (Niedrigkeit, Gemeinheit) – *charity* n.: organization for helping the poor – *solicitor* [səˈlisitə] n.: (here:) professional canvasser (Kundenwerber) for money (for a charity, etc.) – *violate* v.: do harm to (verletzen, Gewalt antun) – *ominous* [ˈɔminəs] a.: announcing evil (unheilkündend, verhängnisvoll) – *kindly* a.: (gütig, liebenswürdig) – *philanthropist* [fiˈlænθrəpist] n.: person who helps others, especially the poor – *the odds are against s.o.*: s.o. is unlikely to succeed – *insuperable* [inˈsjupərəbl] a.: what cannot be overcome (unüberwindlich) – *villain* [ˈvilən] n.: wrongdoer, wicked man – *Moby-Dick*: novel by Herman Melville, published in 1851 (for a brief synopsis of the plot, see the text, ll. 32–41) – *avenge* [əˈvendʒ] v.: (rächen) – *monomaniacal* [ˌmɔnəˈmeinjəkl] a.: having an obsessive interest in one thing to the exclusion of all others – *revenge* n.: (Rache) – *tremendous* a.: very great, enormous – *weld* v.: join (pieces of metal) (zusammenschweißen) – *irresistible* a.: too strong to be resisted – *antagonist* [ˌænˈtægənist] n.: person struggling against another, opponent – *strangle* v.: kill by squeezing the throat of – *loop* v.: (Schlinge, Schlaufe) – *hurl* v.: throw violently – *bizarre* [biˈzɑː] a.: fantastic, strange – *climax* [ˈklaimæks] n.: point of greatest interest or intensity – *environment* n.: surroundings, circumstances, influences (Umgebung) – *Huckleberry Finn*: a novel by Mark Twain, published in 1884 – *subordinate to* a.: less important than – *approve* v.: consider to be right, good, etc. – *hypocrisy* [hiˈpɔkrəsi] n.: (Heuchelei) – *conform* v.: adapt oneself to standards or customs – *core* n.: central or most important part of anything – *generate* [ˈdʒenəreit] v.: cause to exist or occur, produce – *account for s. th.* v.: serve as an explanation of, explain the cause of – *intimate* [ˈintimət] a.: close and familiar –

turmoil ['tə:mɔil] n.: (instance of) trouble – *resolve* [ri'zɔlv] v.: put an end to (difficulties, etc.) by giving an answer – *vanquish* v.: defeat, overcome – *equilibrium* [.ikwi'libriəm] n.: state of being balanced (Gleichgewicht) – *spectacular* [spek'tækjulə] a.: (aufsehenerregend, sensationell) – *illuminate* v.: throw light on.

III. Key terms for detailed field study of words (semantic fields, collocations)

The following terms may be used in order to group systematically the most important word material of the text for more efficient word learning:

1. *language*: use
2. *text*: fiction (story)
3. *text*: fiction (plot)

IV. Suggestions for guided analysis and practice

| Content | The introduction

Analysis

1. How does the writer speak about *plot* in the first printed paragraph (ll. 1–7) as opposed to the paragraphs that follow?
2. How does Stanton group the characteristic elements of *plot* in this paragraph (see 1)?

Practice

3. What is indicated about the listed elements by the repetition of "its" plus nominal group in contrast to "it" plus verbal group with "must/should"? (See ll. 3 and 6.)
4. Considering the "links of cause-and-effect" of plot, how would you illustrate this aspect with the beginning of a *story* that you know?

| Content | The body of the text

Analysis

5. What importance for the four printed paragraphs of the body of the text has the sentence, "The movement of a plot comes chiefly from its ability to arouse questions in our minds ..." (ll. 8f.)?
6. How does Stanton explain this aspect (see 5) in paragraphs 2 and 3 (ll. 8–27; 28–53) in contrast to paragraphs 4 and 5 (ll. 54–72; 73–83)?

Practice

7. Both in connection with "The simplest question" (ll. 9f.) and "The most effective questions" (l. 28) the writer already introduces the term "conflict" (see ll. 11f.: "begins with a violent *conflict* between...", and l. 38: "that this *conflict* is between..."). What does this indicate about the purpose of all these paragraphs?
8. What further aspects of *plot* does Stanton mention when using the plots of Dickens' *A Christmas Carol* and Melville's *Moby-Dick* as illustrations?

| Content | The body of the text

Analysis

9. In his third major paragraph, how does Stanton explain the plot element of *conflict*? Quote relevant parts of his definition.
10. How can the writer's definition be linked with his introductory sentence, "The movement of a plot comes chiefly from its ability to arouse questions in our minds..." (see 5 above)?
11. How does the writer's definition of *climax* link up with his definition of *conflict*?

Practice

12. How would you illustrate *conflict* as an aspect of *plot* from a story that you know?

| Composition |

Analysis

13. As regards *person*, from what point of view does the writer speak in sentences such as the second one (ll. 1–4)?
14. Where else in the text do you find instances of this point of view? Mark the relevant pronouns by underlining.

Practice

15. In the last two paragraphs (ll. 54–83), there is not a single instance of the writer speaking from this point of view (see 13 and 14). How would you account for this against the background of your findings about the first three paragraphs?

| Style |

Analysis

16. Robert Stanton regularly illustrates what his more general statements about *plot* mean. What kind of illustrations are these?

17. In the course of the text, therefore (see 16), the reader might expect Stanton to use *explicatory sequence forms* quite often, as in the sentence, "*As this example illustrates,* a central conflict is always between fundamental and contrasting *qualities* or *forces* [Stanton's italics], *such as* honesty and ..." (ll. 62ff.). What less obvious forms does Stanton use in order to indicate his speaking in a *particularizing* or *exemplifying* manner?

Practice

18. What do these forms (see 17) express?

19. A definition of *illustrative style* reads: "*Illustrative style* is [...] marked by a set of linguistic choices that reflect the encoder's concentration on a concrete linguistic evocation of concepts. Illustrative style is conventionally used among people who lack knowledge and education in a particular field" (see E. Werlich, *A Text Grammar of English,* Heidelberg: Quelle & Meyer, 1976, § 700). How would you support this definition with this text?

15. Jerzy Kosinski, "Documentary photographs"

From: Jerzy Kosinski, *Cockpit.* Bantam Books, 1976 (1975), pp. 206f.

1 While organizing my prints and negatives, I set aside several files for documentary photographs. I often carry a small automatic camera and a couple of extra rolls of film in my pocket. If I happen upon an accident, collision, fire or shoot-out, I snap as many shots as possible and later arrange them into a complete photographic reconstruction
5 of the incident.
Recently I saw a young woman slip while crossing the street, falling directly in the path of an oncoming taxi. Just as she slipped, she screamed, and I raised my camera, getting photos of the entire incident. Her shoulder and neck smashed against the front fender, which dragged her five or six feet. I rushed over to her. While other bystanders tried to
10 comfort her, I began taking pictures from every side. I wanted to establish on film the precise angle and position of the wheels at the moment of the collision, the distance that the woman's body was dragged and the exact nature of the cab's contact with the body. By the time the police and ambulance arrived, I had used three rolls of film. When I told the taxi driver that I had photographed the accident, he said he was
15 anxious to have the prints for his defense. He gave me his name and address, and I promised to contact him. Next, I told the police I had photos of the collision and was eager for the woman's family to see them in case they decided to sue. I was immediately supplied with the name and address of the woman, who at that moment was being lifted into an ambulance.

20 In my apartment, I developed the negatives and enlarged some of the photographs. I selected shots for the cab driver that could best prove his innocence: according to his set, the woman had crossed the street in the middle of the block and tripped because of her high heels. The street surface had been wet, slippery and slightly inclined, and the traces made by the cab's sudden braking indicated it had stayed within its lane.
25 The woman's set of photos, which I mailed to her relatives, suggested she had been hit by a careless driver who hadn't noticed her crossing. It looked as if she had waited on her side of the dividing line for the cab to pass, and had fallen only after its fender had knocked her off balance.

Annotations

print n.: ([Photo]Abzug) – *file* n.: ([Akten]Ordner) – *fender* n.: (Kotflügel) – *defense* n.: (B.E. defence) – *sue* [sju:] n.: (vor Gericht klagen) – *block* n.: (Häuserzeile) – *inclined* a.: (geneigt, abschüssig) – *lane* n.: (Spur, Fahrbahn).

Suggestions for discussion

Interpret this fictional text by making use of relevant concepts for understanding short narratives from the present book.